A-HA!
HOW TO SOLVE ANY PROBLEM
IN RECORD TIME

MARY SCHILLER

Aptitude Consulting, LLC

www.ahabook.biz & www.maryschiller.com

ISBN: 1537245910
ISBN-13: 978-1537245911

DEDICATION

To everyone who feels like life shouldn't be so hard.

CONTENTS

ACKNOWLEDGEMENT

To all the inspiring people I've spoken to these past two years,

thank you.

Introduction:
Not Your Average
Problem-Solving Book

Is it really possible for any problem, even a really big one, to be solved quickly and easily, and without major stress, lengthy "pros and cons" lists or weeks, months or years of agonizing over it?

In a word, *yes*.

What about business problems? Relationship problems? Money problems? Even health problems?

Yes. To everything.

It's not only possible, it's probable – when you know the A-ha! Method described in this book.

You're skeptical, I'm sure. We're only a few sentences into this conversation, so if you're wondering whether you should come along with me, I understand why. After all, who am I to tell you how to solve your problems when I don't even know what they are?

To get the most out of this book, try to set aside what you already know about solving problems. Suspend any judgments about what I might have to say, and then come into the conversation with a completely open mind.

I also encourage you to test everything I tell you. Experiment with it. See for yourself whether this method of problem solving really works, because admittedly, it's different – really different – from everything else out there.

As for me, I know without a doubt that what I've called the A-ha! Method works, and it works 100 percent of the time. How many things can you say that about?

Since you're reading this book, it means that you're stuck in a problem (or maybe several problems). No matter what you do, you can't seem to move forward to a solution. It's almost like there's a force field keeping you standing still, and it may look as though your circumstances are conspiring against you to keep you locked in place.

I know that feeling: as if you're literally frozen, your gaze either fixed in front of you like a laser beam yet seeing nothing useful; or scanning the horizon, frantically searching for something to grab onto.

The problem you're dealing with could be anything from going in circles in your relationships, to struggling with a habit you'd like to break, to trying (and failing) to make more money, to wondering how to have a more fulfilling and less stressful life … anything at all.

You may also be seeing intractable, relentless and repetitive problems in your workplace or in your own business. On Monday, things appear to be all fixed up and ready to go, but by Wednesday, everything seems broken and nonfunctional again. Around and around you go, attending meetings and adjusting processes, firing people and hiring others, reorganizing and restructuring, but the same problems keep showing up. If you're an employee, you're on the receiving end of all this "doing," which is not fun, to say the least.

You're not alone.

Most people seem to believe that certain problems are insoluble, and the best we can do is either learn how to cope with them or figure out how avoid them. Like ... commuting is always going to be a pain in the neck. There's always someone in the family (or the office) who ruins everything for others. Every workplace (or family) has a culture that one has to learn to endure.

You know what I have to say to all of that, and to every other problem that looks like a given?

Horse pucky.

You'll see why, starting in chapter 1.

But before we jump into it – the chapter, not the horse pucky – please take a minute or two (no longer than that) to consider what prompted you to read this book. What problems have you been trying to solve for longer than you'd care to admit? Go ahead and write them here or on another piece of paper, even if it's painful to see them in black and white. No one will peek.

When you finish reading this book, come back here and read what you wrote. If you keep an open mind, I guarantee – yes, guarantee – that this list of problems will look quite different to you.

One other thing: I've made this book intentionally brief and concise because what you'll learn is easy to understand and start using right away. I want you to solve those problems that have been hanging over your head and experience the amazing "a-ha!" Let's go …

CHAPTER 1:
WHAT ARE WE DOING WRONG?

Before I came across what I'll share with you in this book, I was really confused about how to solve problems.

I couldn't figure out why sometimes, solutions would appear as if by magic. In a blinding flash, the answer would come to me "out of the blue," as they say. Everyone has had that happen to them at one time or another. The shower seems to be a favorite place for most people's "a-ha!" moments, including me. Other times, though, I would struggle for weeks, months, even years – and never find a satisfactory answer to a problem or even an appropriate next step to take. I'd get stuck.

Does that sound familiar?

As it turned out, my real problem wasn't the problem itself. It was that I didn't understand what I was doing right when solutions appeared effortlessly, and what I was doing wrong – innocently wrong, but still wrong – when no matter what I tried, I couldn't see my way clear to an answer.

There's a reason why we bounce back and forth between these two extremes.

We actually have a built-in, 100-percent reliable system that can help us solve any problem, big or small, in record time. The trouble is …

1) this system is invisible to us, and
2) no one has ever taught us how to access it.

In just a moment, I'll walk you through the simple steps to use this powerful, innate problem-solving system so that you can have those "a-ha!" realizations anytime you need them.

First, though, I'd like to see if you can write out your current problem-solving process. You may never have thought about what you're doing when you solve problems, but give it a go. For instance, does a problem occupy your thoughts for hours or days on end until you simply must make a decision – and you do so in a stressed-out state of mind? Do you methodically plot out the pros and cons on paper? Do you go with your gut instinct? Write out your typical problem-solving process here or on another piece of paper.

Most problem-solving methods out there seem to have one thing in common: they are impossible to follow! Do a quick Google search and you'll see what I mean. For example, I came across one problem-solving method that had 10 steps, with the final one being, "Just go out and solve your problem." What?

Another wildly popular blog suggested that I simplify the problem (although it didn't tell me how to do that), create a plan with action steps, but then make the plan really flexible so that I didn't have to follow the steps ('huh?).

Luckily, there's a much, much better way to solve problems that involves only two simple – and unforgettable – steps.

As for me, I deal with the typical day-to-day problems most of us have, like bad drivers, wonky wi-fi, sour milk. But up until 2014, I had two areas of my life that I considered to be really B-I-G problems: money and marriage.

Let's start with a quick trip to Mary's Money Freak-out Land.

For many years – at least twenty, if I'm honest about it – I would get extremely nervous if I had to confront anything related to money, like doing my taxes or finding ways to increase my income. It was a real struggle for me to approach money with any sort of clarity. I also felt like I had missed this particular lesson in life, because it seemed like everyone else knew how to "do money" better than I did.

For example, let's say I ran into a cash flow problem: the worst of all possible situations, as far as I was concerned. When I say I freaked out, I mean I *really* freaked out.

I didn't sleep. My mind was consumed with thoughts of, "What if I can't pay the bills? What if I can't get any more money coming in the door? What if I lose my home? I need to fix this problem right now! Do something, Mary!"

Underneath it all was a core belief that if I didn't focus on the problem, my worst nightmares of homelessness and ruin would come true. I'd wake up every morning with money foremost on my mind after getting little sleep.

It was torture.

At one point in 2013, I spent a fair amount of money – oh, the irony – on a coaching program to change my money mindset and finally get a grip on this money thing. I wanted to make a whole lot more money and, naturally, worry about money a whole lot less. I figured if I had more money, there'd be less to worry about!

So when this money expert told me I should write down every penny I spent for an entire month, I did it. When she told me to search my house for coins and put them in a jar and count them, I did it. When she told me to have $200 in my wallet at all times so that I didn't feel poor, I did it.

I was obsessed with improving the way I thought about money: looking at where my money beliefs came from (my parents, naturally), seeing how I could change those beliefs and celebrating little money successes ("Oh, I found a dollar bill on the subway platform!") ... you get the idea. There were also positive affirmations I recited about my self-worth, my value to the world and my relationship to money. I listened to subliminal message recordings, the whole thing.

All of this activity and learning was supposed to help me have the money I needed without so much effort – the way I saw lots of other people living, and what I craved for myself. Seems logical, doesn't it?

It didn't work. A year later, I was still freaked out about money and had no more in my bank account, either. And was I ever mad about that. Why couldn't I change my thinking about money enough to make more of it and make it less of a big deal? Why couldn't I "attract" money the way other people did, instead of apparently "repelling" it? I mean, was it my antiperspirant, or what? My money problems seemed permanent. I didn't know how to fix them.

I was also riding
Mary's Marriage Merry-Go-Round.

My husband and I got married in 1997, and we began to have problems around 2006, culminating with a separation for several months in 2011-2012. As I'm writing this book in 2016, we're happily married (hooray!), but for a long time we were really struggling, culminating in that separation and some events I'd rather not remember.

Being the person that I am, I tried everything I could think of to save my marriage. I loved my husband, and I knew he loved me. But things just weren't working between us at all.

We went to counseling, which actually seemed to make things worse. I bought an expensive (see a trend here?) marriage fix-it program from a marriage-mending guru, consisting of books, workbooks, DVDs and audios. Every moment of the day I wasn't worrying about money I was worrying about my marriage. Those two topics consumed nearly all my thoughts as I tried to figure out what to do.

With both my money and my marriage, there were times when I would just sit down, completely frustrated, and say, "Today is the day that I solve this problem. I'm going to write out a bunch of ideas and start trying each one until something works. I've had it!"

So that's what I did. Related to my marriage, I'd think to myself, "What could he and I do differently in terms of interacting with each other? Maybe we need to go out on dates again or take more weekends away."

I would come up with plans and more plans. We almost never followed through on them, and our marriage continued to list, like a boat without a sail.

And still, I'd start every day with the same thought: "What can I do to fix my marriage?" Usually followed closely by, "What can I do to make more money?"

It's incredibly disheartening to wake up day after day with the same problems hanging over your head and wondering, "What am I doing wrong?"

After a while, it seems like these problems are part of your life and part of you, and the answer is either to accept that as fact or, in the case of a relationship, potentially end it.

Over the years, some psychotherapists, and also well-meaning friends and family members, had told me that there were certain things in life that we simply had to accept. Once we reached that point of acceptance, we could move on somehow, and that was the best we could do.

With money, I tried to accept that I'd always be stressed about it, I'd never have enough and I'd never be able to manage it well. I just didn't "get it."

With my marriage, I remember thinking, "OK, maybe this is as good as it's ever going to be for us, and I should just be grateful that we're together and have a reasonably happy life."

But you know what?

That all sounded like horse pucky! (I like using the word "pucky," can you tell?)

The trouble was, I couldn't figure out what else to do.

I stayed on the money and marriage merry-go-rounds for years, trying this, that and the other thing but always coming around to the same place: stuck.

I didn't know then what I know now — what you're about to discover in the next chapter, coming right up …

CHAPTER 2:
THE A-HA! METHOD, STEP 1

The A-ha! Method is not like anything you've seen before. If you're expecting empirical research or academic citations, or if you're looking for the typical how-to steps that you'll find in other books about problem solving, you're out of luck.

This is a good thing! You want something new, right? Something that actually works – and can work quickly?

I thought so. You're about to discover how to generate those "a-ha!" solutions to even big life problems more and more often, with zero effort.

Let's begin with this question: What are some areas of your life that come easily to you? Describe them here or on a separate piece of paper. Don't be shy. This is the place for bragging, so go for it. Write out what activities you enjoy that seem effortless, or life situations that rarely seem like obstacles for you but can be difficult for other people, like health, money and so forth.

One area of ease for me is my weight. I've never had a problem with my weight and have never been on a diet (rare for an American woman, I suspect). The one time I needed to lose weight – I gained the "Freshman 15" during my first year of college – I did so easily, with no effort whatsoever. I simply made a decision to avoid sugar and processed foods for three months, and the extra weight vanished, never to return.

I almost never think about food. I never think about what I've eaten, nor do I really plan what I'm going to eat. The whole topic of "food" occupies nearly zero space in my thoughts, except when I feel hungry and realize it's time for me to eat lunch.

This question kept coming to mind: "Why is it so easy for me to manage my weight, but money and my marriage are such big problems?"

So let me ask you this: In the area or areas of your life that come easily to you, what do you notice about them? Do they have anything in common? Write out a few ideas here or on a separate piece of paper.

You may already be seeing one of the secrets behind the A-ha! Method of problem solving, but there's an important twist that is essential. Keep paying close attention, and I'll let you know when you run across something that is worth a second (or third) read.

With money and my marriage, I believed that if I focused on the problem and gave it a lot of presence in my mind, I'd find the answer.

I was making a mistake. An innocent mistake, but still a mistake. And it's one I'll bet you're making, too. As intuitive as it may seem, focusing our attention on a problem, taking it apart and then trying to create a solution is actually the least effective way to solve it.

A couple of years ago, I came across a new understanding of how the mind works that forms the basis of the A-ha! Method of problem solving. As a result, I started to experience a completely different way of seeing problems and finding great solutions – or at least great next steps.

Let's go back to Mary's Marriage Merry-Go-Round as an example ...

When I began looking more closely at my relationship, I noticed that sometimes, my marriage seemed great. I had warm feelings toward my husband and about the life we had created together. On those days, it didn't look like I had any marital problems at all. But other days, it looked to me like I had real problems – B-I-G problems. We didn't talk enough. We were on other sides of the world emotionally, despite living in the same 600-square-foot apartment together. We didn't act like a team, which is something I really wanted in my relationship.

I'd see all these things that were wrong … but then sometimes, I didn't see them at all.

I asked myself some key questions, like these:

1) Did my feelings about my marriage depend on something I was doing?

2) Did my feelings about my marriage depend on something my husband was doing?

The answer to both of those questions, I soon realized, was an emphatic *no*. For instance, my husband could be complaining about work, and one day I'd find it insanely annoying, and the next day I'd find myself having great compassion for him. I wasn't doing anything differently, and neither was he. My feelings simply were what they were. What accounted for that?

Then I began to wonder whether all the focusing, worrying, planning and trying was having any positive effect at all. Clearly, the answer to that was also *no*. If all that effort had been helping things, my money and marriage problems would have disappeared a long time ago.

Here's where you need to pay close attention, because this applies to you, too. After lots of experimenting, here's what I found out:

1) The only thing that made a difference in how I saw my problems was my state of mind at any given time – not what I did, nor what anyone else did.

2) I couldn't control my state of mind or my thoughts no matter how hard I tried, and my state of mind actually improved when I stopped trying to control it.

Whoa! Wait a minute. What did I just say?

I'll put it another way. I discovered that my state of mind was the only variable in what I was experiencing, whether it was money, my marriage or any other circumstance or situation (whether it looked problematic or not).

This was an absolute revelation to me.

Never in my life had I stopped to consider that problems could exist or not exist based solely on whatever thinking was going through my brain at any given time. Since my thoughts seemed pretty random, I also realized that I didn't have to engage with whatever thoughts I had.

Even more revelatory, I saw that my state of mind changed for the better the less I interfered with it.

I couldn't believe it. When I let go of the steering wheel, so to speak, my state of mind straightened out all on its own.

Here is how this new way of seeing things played out in my marriage. When I'd notice myself getting worked up about something, and it looked like a big problem that had to be solved, I did nothing.

That's right: I did nothing.

I didn't talk about it – whatever "it" happened to be in that moment. I stayed quiet. I didn't try to come up with lists of ideas, nor did I take any action. I felt whatever I felt in the moment and didn't do anything at all. Even if the feeling was uncomfortable, I still did nothing to try to change it – and surprisingly, the uncomfortable feeling faded away on its own, and fast.

I understand that what I'm saying is really different from everything you've heard before, particularly about solving problems in a relationship, but please stay with me here. When I felt like something was blowing up and my insides were getting all scrambled, I recognized that it was not the time to talk with my husband, make a decision or take any sort of action. I waited it out.

Not only that, but I also stopped looking for answers from other people, like friends, family or marriage "experts," and I quit looking for solutions even in my own thinking.

Yes, you read that correctly.

I stopped looking to my own thinking for solutions.

I realized that if I had had a certain thought before, it was stale and of no use to me. The answers I needed weren't there. No combination of old ideas was going to bring about a new idea. Every time I heard an old thought, I simply said, "Heard you before. Next!"

You may be asking, "Mary, what do you mean? If the answers aren't in my own thinking, where the heck are they?" I love that question, and I'll answer it in just a second.

Unbeknownst to me, in recognizing that a) my state of mind was the only variable in how I experienced things in my life, including problems, and b) that the answers weren't in my old thinking, I had discovered what I now call the A-ha! Method of problem solving.

Are you ready to try it for yourself? It's only two simple steps, so let's begin with …

Step 1: Take a time-out.

Most of us look at our problems, big and small, and our breath catches in our throat. We feel nervous, and we might get really scared. We believe we have to dive straight into them, especially if they seem super-duper important and super-duper, "hair-on-fire" urgent.

Don't do it. Mentally step back and sit down on an imaginary bench inside your head, no matter how uncomfortable it may be for you to do that.

I'm not talking about ignoring problems. This is different.

If you have any sense of urgency in relation to a problem – whether it's a tiny tingling in your forehead or a prodigious pit in your stomach – take a time-out.

I know this seems counter-intuitive, but when you feel worked up and stressed, it means you have some intense thinking happening in that moment that's clouding your ability to see what to do. You're not going to find a solution when you're in that stressed-out state of mind. The familiar voice in your head is not telling you anything helpful.

I also know it can really look like the problem itself, whatever it may be, is causing this intense and even terrifying feeling you're experiencing. Even though it looks that way, it's not true.

That's a brain twister and worth another look.

We're never experiencing the "thing." We're always experiencing our thinking about the thing, so our feelings are coming from thoughts, not from the thing itself.

And even the thing itself – whatever it is – might actually be a creation of our thinking.

Did you catch that last statement? Talk about a game changer!

For instance, when I would go through the turnstile and into Mary's Money Freak-out Land, riding the ups and downs of the rollercoasters there, I wasn't experiencing "money." I was actually experiencing my up-and-down thinking about money. And in fact, "money" itself was a creation of my thinking!

All those freaked-out feelings were coming from thoughts, not from money. Because how could a feeling come from anything but myself?

That's a lot of thinking going on. So do you see now why it's good for you to take a compassionate time-out to let your thoughts settle? If what we're experiencing is our thoughts, then allowing them to calm down is the best way for us to calm down, too. Then we'll actually be in a great place to find an answer (more on that in step 2).

Don't try to change or get rid of the worked-up, scary feeling. There's no need. It will change on its own as soon as your thoughts change. It's how we're designed, to settle down naturally. You know that built-in system I was talking about before? This ability to regain our composure is a big part of it, and it works faster if we don't do anything to try to hasten it.

I can't begin to tell you what a difference this simple step of taking a time-out has made, not only in terms of finding answers to questions and problems, but also to the quality of my life.

I'm no longer following the white rabbit running through my mind telling me I need to *hurry up! hurry up!* and find an answer. Instead, I'm seeing the rabbit running around and I'm saying, "You know what? I don't want to follow you right now. I'm going to bench myself for a bit, instead."

In my relationship with my husband, I started testing what happened when I took a time-out. I'd have a lot of stress and anger because I was listening to thoughts telling me something horrible about my marriage, like "Why can't he really listen to me for once, instead of ignoring me? I'm so sick of this!"

When I'd feel myself getting worked up, I would simply take a time-out. That was all I did. Every time a thought about my husband came to mind that I really didn't want to have because it brought with it a negative feeling, I took a mental time-out and ignored the thought. I noticed that the less I paid attention to old, heard-it-before thinking, the easier life became for me.

Over time, I was shocked to see that problems between us started to dissolve without any effort. The day-to-day marital discord that I had assumed would always be there suddenly wasn't. We had our moments, but they were fleeting.

Ironically – or perhaps not – he and I used to argue a lot about our finances. I noticed that my stress around money started to fade, and then our disagreements about money were gradually replaced by more ease. If something came up related to money that we did need to deal with, we were in a much better emotional and mental place to allow the solution to appear (hint: that's in step 2).

Whew, take a deep breath here.

That first step alone can make all the difference in the world and has a lot of really amazing implications. Let's summarize what we've seen so far.

1) The only variable that determines how we see problems is our state of mind -- because we're experiencing our thinking, not the "thing" we're thinking about.

2) We can't control our state of mind, which is great because it takes a big item off of our "to do" list.

3) We regain composure quickly – our state of mind improves – if we take a time-out and allow our thoughts to settle down at the first hint of stress.

4) The less we pay attention to old, stale thinking (that familiar voice inside our heads), the more easily we see solutions, even to longstanding problems.

Remember, I really want you
to experiment with this for yourself.

The next time you feel worked up over something that seems like a big problem, take a time-out. Do nothing to try to change the situation or the feeling, even if it's uncomfortable. What do you notice? Write about your experience here or on another piece of paper.

Now, let's explore the second step in the A-ha! Method ...

CHAPTER 3:
THE A-HA! METHOD, STEP 2

You may be starting to see that the A-ha! Method of problem solving is all about *not doing*. Instead of all the *doing*, it's about understanding the system we already have in place within us and allowing it to do its thing – instead of innocently throwing wrenches into the gears because we don't know how the engine runs.

When you follow step 1 and simply take a time-out, something truly miraculous happens. And the best part is, it's automatic. You're not actually doing it consciously; the built-in system is doing it for you.

When that feeling of stress is lifted by taking a brief time-out and allowing thoughts to settle down naturally, it's like the blinders fall away. You know that sense of tunnel vision I mentioned earlier, or the frantic searching where your inner eye is darting in a million directions but seeing nothing helpful? That activity dissipates effortlessly and is replaced by our natural state, which is one of clarity, creativity and well-being.

Let me repeat that: our natural state is one of clarity, creativity and well-being.

Most of us unwittingly believe that through combining and recombining old ideas, we're going to find the new answer we need. So we spend a lot of time focusing, focusing, focusing and searching, searching, searching. I picture someone scrounging through old file folders they've looked through a thousand times already, hoping that they'll see something new and different.

This is not an effective way to solve any problem, let alone a big problem.

Instead, allow step 2 to happen naturally: Wait for the "a-ha!"

I can hear you now ...

"Mary, did you just skip a few steps? Did I miss something?"

Don't go flipping back through the pages of this book. You didn't miss anything. And remember, you don't even have to take this second step actively, because it will happen on its own once you take that time-out.

Our thoughts are designed to settle like dust after a sudden storm. As the storm passes, everything that was churned up goes back to its natural state of rest. With the air cleared, we can see where we are. Our vision becomes sharper as well as wider, instead of darting and panicky. A strong and confident presence of mind takes over.

And then, we're primed for that irresistibly beautiful feeling: "A-ha!"

We might realize, for example, that this "urgent" problem we have can be taken care of by someone else. Perhaps it doesn't need to be dealt with at all, or certainly not right this minute. Or an answer will become so obvious, we'll wonder why we didn't see it sooner.

Often it's as if we've woken up in a whole new landscape of opportunity, and ideas are flourishing everywhere we look.

A perfect example for me of the A-ha! Method's effectiveness happened in early 2016.

My husband and I were surprised by several unexpected – and large – bills that we had to pay. Just imagine: this situation combined both of my B-I-G life problems all in one!

When we heard the news, for about two to three minutes we were both unbelievably stressed.

Not two to three days, not two to three hours. Just two to three minutes. In the past, for me it would have been more like two or three months.

Now I will tell you, those were not the most pleasant few minutes. We were both in a freaked-out and scared state of mind: "This is a disaster! What are we going to do? Could this have happened at a worse time?" Our hearts and minds were racing a mile a minute.

But then we realized what was happening: we were both caught up in some momentary – key word here, *momentary* – thinking. We said to each other non-verbally, just by looking into each other's eyes, "We don't have to listen to all that stressful, urgent thinking, do we? We can step back and take a time-out."

So that's what we did. We both got quiet and didn't say anything for about thirty minutes. We sat with the uncomfortable feeling until it faded away.

And then, we had a new idea. Interestingly, we both came to the same, exact conclusion about what to do. Crazy, right?

We didn't know for sure if the potential solution was viable, so we made a couple of calls to see If it could work. Surprisingly, all signs pointed to "yes."

Within an hour, we had a potentially great solution to a problem that in those first few minutes looked absolutely disastrous. For me, this was a poignant example of how the A-ha! Method works in real life, not just in theory.

When my husband and I allowed our thinking to settle down, it took just a few minutes for us to see where we actually were: in a life filled with possibility and solutions. We did step 1 and step 2 of the A-ha! Method without effort, and an answer appeared almost instantaneously.

Is a solution always going to come that quickly? No, but it will appear as soon as you see that your state of mind is the cause of your distress and not the "thing" you're stressing over.

Here's another important point: People can really get tripped up when they believe that if they take their eye off the ball, the big problem is not going to get solved. They believe the problem will just get bigger and bigger and out of control.

I used to be that way. I believed that if I wasn't focused on a money problem, for example, I'd have to deal with it later, and it would be a bigger mess than ever. Especially related to my finances, I always felt that if I wasn't hyper-vigilant about everything, it would all disintegrate. And I would disintegrate along with it.

What I have come to see, instead, is that the less I give any weight to thoughts like, "This is a big problem!" or "This is really serious!" the more easily potential answers come to me. I'm sitting in that time-out, knowing that I don't have to pay attention to that kind of thinking. And before I know it, the "a-ha!" moment has arrived.

I can't jump into a summary of this chapter without first mentioning the incredibly beautiful feeling that comes with "a-ha!" How would you describe it? Write out your answer here or on another piece of paper.

An insight, a new idea, a fresh thought, a potential solution: they all bring with them a wonderfully good feeling. There is no hint of stress or strain. No worries about what the outcome will be. You just *know*, you know?

The cool thing is, you don't have to get the entire, soup-to-nuts answer in that immediate "a-ha!" It's enough to see the next small step you can take. Other times, you might actually see a whole plan laid out in front of you.

If you find yourself second-guessing an "a-ha!" realization, most likely those second thoughts are not trustworthy and are simply well-worn thoughts you've had thousands of times before. No fresh ideas can be found in old thoughts, so listen to the "a-ha!" with confidence.

Even though we're just a few chapters into this book, we've covered a lot of ground. Let's do a quick review of the simple two-step A-ha! Method of problem solving.

Step 1: Take a time-out.

When something looks like a pressing, scary problem that you have to solve *right now, or else!* you are allowed to step back from that thinking. Your thoughts are swirling like a dust storm, so do nothing, sit with the uncomfortable feeling and allow your thoughts to settle.

The less you do to try to change the feeling, the quicker you'll feel calm again.

With this step, you're taking advantage of a built-in system designed to return you to your natural state of composure, clarity and well-being.

Step 2: Wait for the "a-ha!"

After the dust settles, the air around you is clear again. Space opens up. That space is ready and waiting for a new thought – an insight – to rush in and help you. This is your best opportunity to experience an "a-ha!" If you're still feeling stressed, go back to step 1 and give it more time.

Chances are, unless you're about to get hit by a speeding train, you don't need the answer to a problem right this very second. Allow the system to work as its designed, and the solution will come to you when you need it.

Take a moment here to consider what you've read so far. What I'm describing is something that's already part of you.

It's how you are designed: to be able to access resources, answers and inner resilience naturally, without doing anything at all.

I don't know about you, but knowing that I have a built-in problem-solving system that I can access anytime, anywhere makes living life a whole lot less stressful – and a lot less problematic.

In the next chapter, we'll explore how the A-ha! Method of problem solving can have a major positive impact on life and work. We'll also see why this system we've been talking about is so much better than other methods of solving problems in terms of results …

CHAPTER 4:
THE A-HA! METHOD IN ACTION

In this chapter, we'll talk about why the A-ha! Method works so perfectly in any situation, be it in your professional life or in your personal life.

Let's start with the workplace.

If you have ever held a job or run a company, you have undoubtedly been in a meeting where the focus was on solving a problem. Think back for a moment to how those meetings were run. There may have been someone standing in front of a white board, jotting down ideas as people brainstormed possible solutions. Perhaps the meeting ended with action items – or maybe, like most meetings, it ended with a bunch of ideas on a whiteboard with no solid plan for what to do next.

More often than not, people in these meetings will come up with a short-term fix that may look like a permanent solution, but it usually doesn't turn out that way. Before long, people are back in the same old circular thinking patterns and behavior, and the problem remains the same or even worse.

I admit, for most of my life I didn't understand why these kinds of meetings produced such flat results. I mean, we have a lot of smart people sitting in a room together, all focused on one problem we're trying to solve, our brains active and contributing ideas. So why aren't we able to come up with a real, viable answer?

That way of solving problems seemed like the right thing to do at the time, but now, I see that it's upside down and backwards, for all the reasons you and I have been exploring in this book.

As I see it today, there are two major things wrong with this typical scenario that plays out thousands – maybe millions – of times a day in workplaces around the world.

1) People do not understand that focusing on a problem is the worst way to find a truly effective solution.

As we've seen so far, more thinking doesn't bring about the best answer. Remember my example about my weight? And remember what you noted about yourself in terms of what comes easily to you? We don't have a lot of noisy thinking in those areas. The voice inside our head is pretty quiet.

Effective problem solving involves listening for something that's beyond our thoughts, beyond the voice in our head – to new ideas and insights that appear when our thinking fades into the background.

Honestly, nothing would please me more than to see workplaces ban "brainstorming sessions." By design, they go against this built-in system that produces those "a-ha!" realizations that are naturally available to us. Every brainstorming session I've ever been a part of has attempted to corral and harness people's thinking, but that's not where the answer is. Even when people come up with new ideas during these sessions, they are not nearly as effective as they could be. That brings me to this key point …

2) If people in the workplace understood how this built-in problem-solving system works and how to access it easily, solutions would be much more leveraged, and businesses would save time and money, not to mention employee stress.

When we take a time-out and wait for the "a-ha!", what is delivered is an answer tailored specifically to us and to the question we have. It's almost as if we're tapping into a never-ending stream of wisdom that has our name on it.

I'll give you a funny example. Recently, I found myself struggling in a certain area related to my coaching business. It was a Sunday night, and I remember having that dizzying, merry-go-round sensation. My thoughts were loud and insistent, telling me I needed to solve this particular problem immediately.

So I took a time-out. Right away, I realized that I didn't have to follow the frantic thoughts, and I let that feeling of urgency wash over me like a wave. As I went to sleep in a peaceful state of mind, I said to myself, "I'd love to wake up tomorrow with some new ideas about what to do."

I awoke Monday morning – this is absolutely true – and I saw two emails in my inbox from friends of mine. One friend had written the email at 6 a.m., and in it she said, "I woke up this morning with a fantastic idea about promoting your business. Can we talk today?"

The other email was from another friend of mine who had a brilliant idea about a business opportunity that we could pursue together.

I cracked up! I thought, "OK, I asked for some new ideas, but that doesn't mean they have to be my own, I guess!"

That's what I was referring to earlier when I said that sometimes, problems can get solved without us intervening and taking action. Both of those ideas were viable, and as I'm writing this book, I'm pursuing them and seeing where they might lead.

When we understand that our default setting is clarity, and when we can see that our old and stale thoughts don't hold the solution we need, we're able to take advantage of this problem-solving system we've been given as human beings.

Anytime we want to, we can take a time-out and fall back into that beautiful, clear spaciousness – where opportunities that may have been available to us all along become apparent.

In my previous example, if I been super stressed and worried when I read those two emails, I might have said, "I can't do that. That doesn't seem worth talking about or even exploring." But I was calm and open to whatever came to me.

Most of us don't realize that it's not always up to us to have the answers.

Not everything is on our shoulders. We can say a gentle "no" to that urgent, stressful thinking and realize that we have at our disposal an infinite number of possible solutions: even solutions that may come to us in the form of another person.

I've also found that saying "I don't know" can clear the smoke quickly. That phrase can be powerful because it essentially halts all that noisy thinking and launches us into a state of mind that's ready to hear something new.

Now, let's get personal.

I solved the biggest problem of my life by understanding what I've been sharing with you in this book. For thirty years, I suffered from the symptoms of post-traumatic stress disorder. I was anxious, I'd have emotional outbursts, and while I had some happy times and enjoyed certain aspects of my life, the overall quality of my daily experience was fair to poor.

What I didn't understand back then was that my suffering was coming from listening to stressful, urgent thinking. As soon as I realized this, I simply took a time-out anytime I felt anxious or scared. For example, someone would be standing close to me on the subway – a normal daily occurrence – and I'd have the thought of "That person might hurt me!" Instead of giving that thought a lot of weight, I didn't worry about having that thought or the anxious feeling that came with it. I'd sit with the feeling, however uncomfortable it was, and I'd wait it out.

In a few minutes, the anxious thoughts and their attendant feelings would move along, and I'd find myself in that state of spaciousness, where anything and everything looked possible. Within six weeks, my symptoms of PTSD were gone completely, never to return. I was astonished at that result, considering the 25+ psychotherapists I'd seen over the years and countless techniques I had tried to get rid of PTSD. That's when I knew for sure that no problem was too big to solve with the A-ha! Method. I realized that if it could help me, it could help anyone.

In my work with clients, I have seen people solve big life problems so fast, I almost couldn't believe it: dissolving a decade of depression within six months; gaining the courage to pursue their passions – like writing, photography, music and art – instead of letting them languish anymore; eliminating years of regret and beginning to mend a fractured family relationship in just a few weeks' time; and many, many more.

The more time you spend in a state of ease instead of stress, the more freedom you experience to do the things that you want to do and live the life you want to live. Answers to problems come to you more readily, and they bring that glorious "a-ha!" feeling along with them instead of a sense of resigned acceptance. Not only that, but problems themselves start to transform into something completely different. More on this amazing feature coming up in the next chapter …

CHAPTER 5:
THE REAL SECRET OF THE A-HA! METHOD

If you're one of those people who has jumped to this chapter because you like to read the ending first, well, I forgive you. But you may want to go back through the rest of this short book before reading this part because otherwise, it won't make complete sense.

Earlier, I mentioned that I had never stopped to consider that problems could exist, or not exist, based on whatever my state of mind was at any given time. I had always seen problems as problems, many of which seemed to have no solutions – or at least, I couldn't find them.

After experimenting with the A-ha! Method, I came upon a new thought, myself.

Is there anything that can really be called a "problem"? Or does something only look like a problem depending on what thoughts I happen to have?

I'll give you a personal example of when I realized that a problem isn't necessarily a problem.

As I'm writing this book, I have spent the last year going through a "wait and see" process related to some cancer testing. The first time I went in for the test and then waited for the results, I felt sick to my stomach with anxiety. When they told me I had to come back in a few months and get checked again before they could give me a definitive answer, I felt some stress, but it faded quickly. The next time I went in for the testing, I was completely calm – even though the situation was exactly the same. I had a potential "health problem." I was re-doing the test and, once again, awaiting the result: was it cancer, or was it benign?

But that final time, I had no nausea, no stress, nothing. I was totally relaxed. How is that possible?

It's because my feelings – just like yours – come from whatever momentary thinking I have. I could see this cancer testing as a "health problem," or I could see it as neutral if I wasn't listening to any stressful thinking related to it. (The results were benign, by the way.)

Not long ago, I attended a series of talks where the topic was how our state of mind really works – just like I've been sharing with you in this book. I'll never forget what one of the participants said after hearing this for himself.

He said, "I've realized that the worst thing I'll ever experience in life is some unpleasant thinking."

Did you catch that? The only thing we're ever up against in life is our own state of mind.

That bears repeating: The only thing we're ever up against in life is our own state of mind.

Does that seem real to you? Or does it look like there are all kinds of problems and obstacles in your life? If it's the latter, start looking at them a bit more closely. Before long, you'll begin to see that what looks real is actually a product of whatever your thoughts are at any given moment.

We're not up against our circumstances or other people. We're not up against what look like "problems." We're only ever dealing with our own state of mind. Fortunately, as you've seen so far, our state of mind is designed to settle back into composure and clarity if we do nothing to try to change it.

I'll go back to my example of money. When I took a time-out whenever I felt stressed about money, I saw through the illusion of my own thinking about it. My eyes then opened to opportunities that were previously invisible to me. I launched a brand new career, started coaching people, and began writing and publishing books like this one.

I'm also not listening anymore when my thinking tells me something is a crisis. For instance, if I need more income to pay unexpected bills, I've discovered, after taking a time-out, that actually I have enough money; it's somewhere, and I can find it. The "crisis" was all the "what if" futuristic scenarios my thoughts were showing me – like a movie. They weren't real.

Remember how I asked you to experiment and try this for yourself? That's exactly what I did.

I'd be feeling stressed and worried, and I'd take a time-out. Questions would come to me, like, "Do I really have to deal with this problem right now? What would happen if I didn't respond to that stressful thinking and waited it out?"

Time after time, I saw something truly unbelievable: the horribly scary, important problem wasn't actually a horribly scary, important problem about 99.9 percent of the time.

There was no big, ugly problem hanging over me. There was no crisis. There was nothing that needed to be solved urgently. When I took a time-out and my thoughts settled down, I saw that what looked like something I had to take care of right then and there was actually no such thing.

Since our state of mind changes constantly, and it's designed to return to clarity when our thoughts settle down, is there ever really a problem – even with our thinking? The way I see it, the answer is *no*.

Thoughts themselves are not the problem.

They do what they do; they come and go, and they bring feelings and experiences along with them. Sometimes those feelings and experiences look like problems, and sometimes they don't – which seems to indicate, at least to me, that "problems" don't actually exist at all.

It can be really interesting to observe that a problem at 8 a.m. can be forgotten by 9 a.m. My mood, like yours, changes multiple times during the day because my thoughts are constantly changing. Things will look urgent and important ... and then they won't.

Are you also starting to realize that if much of what we see as a "problem" is really momentary thinking, then looking to our thinking is not the best way to solve problems? That's why we can have the sensation of being stuck in an endless loop.

As always, I invite you to experiment with all of this. For example, see if you can spot times during your day where you're in the same, exact circumstance but your experience of things is quite different. What accounts for that? It's your fluctuating state of mind.

Go back to that list of problems you wrote in the introduction. Do they look any different to you after reading this book? Do they still seem like true problems? If they do, are you now seeing a different way to solve them? I'll leave a little room here in case you'd like to make some notes.

Pretty soon, it might dawn on you – as it did for me – that no matter how things may look to you, everything is actually OK. You're here. You're breathing. Your natural state, as you and I have talked about, is one of clarity, composure, creativity and mental well-being. How might your life change if you didn't see problems the same way anymore, and instead, your days were filled with ease and the beautiful "a-ha!" feeling more often? Write out how that would be for you.

For me, this realization has produced a sense of freedom beyond my wildest dreams. I'm no longer afraid to say "yes" to ideas and opportunities that come to me in those "a-ha!" moments because I trust them, and I trust myself.

That kind of life – freedom from problems and a feeling, instead, of expansiveness and possibility – is not only possible for you, it's what you already have … in every single "a-ha!"

You must have questions, so I'll provide answers …

CHAPTER 6:
FREQUENTLY ASKED QUESTIONS

Q. Is the A-ha! Method of problem solving anything like the Law of Attraction or other self-development or self-help tools and techniques?

A. No. All you need "do" is see that your momentary thinking is creating your experience of a stressful problem. Once you take a brief time-out, that stressful thinking starts to settle down, the stress fades away, and the "a-ha!" moment is just around the corner.

We also don't have to attract good feelings and abundance into our lives. Why would we have to attract something that we already have? The answer is that we don't. We already have everything, and the answers we need are right here. When we start to experience our natural state of clarity more often, we see how many resources already exist within us to solve any problem at all.

Q. Did you come up with the the A-ha! Method all on your own, Mary?

A. The A-ha! Method is my interpretation of the insights of Sydney Banks and his expression of those insights as the Three Principles of Mind, Consciousness and Thought. Since I have personally seen how much those principles have helped me solve problems, I wanted to create a simple way for other people to see it for themselves. So I developed the A-ha! Method to try to help.

Q. What really makes the A-ha! Method so different?

A. Despite the fact that it has two "steps," it is not prescriptive. It is not telling us to do anything active; in fact, it's just the opposite. It's showing us this built-in system of problem solving that's already at work, and we can access it anytime we need it just by knowing that it exists. It couldn't be any simpler.

Q. Can the A-ha! Method help with problems like bad habits or addictions?

A. Yes. Even those problems, believe it or not, come from listening to stressful thinking. For example, let's look at someone who smokes. They are attempting to solve the problem of their discomfort and stress by reaching for a cigarette. But how can a cigarette do anything to help with momentary thoughts, which are the real cause of the person's distress? The answer is, it can't. It's like going to a dentist when you have a broken leg.

When people see that they can wait a few moments and let the distressed thinking pass on by, as it's designed to do, the need to try to force it to go away vanishes, too. And it also becomes obvious that anything on the "outside" – like a cigarette – has no relationship whatsoever to easing our discomfort. The good feeling we have that might come at the same time we smoke a cigarette is actually coming from within ourselves, not from the cigarette. Now that's what I call a big "a-ha!"

Q. Is there more for me to learn about the A-ha! Method?

A. The principles that form the foundation of the A-ha! Method offer endless possibilities for exploration. For me, that's the best part. The rest of my life will be an exciting journey into that exciting "a-ha!" feeling that's available to us in any moment.

Q. The A-ha! Method makes it look like I'm not doing anything to solve problems. Is that right?

A. Yes, that's right. The answer you need is already within you. It's simply a matter of knowing how to allow the built-in system to "do its thing" without interference. In other words, even though you're not aware of it, you possess an automatic problem-solving machine that's at work every minute of every day. Allow your stressful, problem-based thinking to pass on by, and the answer will become clear.

Q. If I understand the A-ha! Method, does that mean I'll never have a problem again?

A. You'll still have times when things look like problems. We have thoughts; those thoughts instantly create certain feelings, like fear and worry.

But here's the difference: you don't need to be concerned about having those feelings because they're simply reflecting your thinking in the moment, and that's all. Your feelings don't mean anything more than that. They're not a reflection of who you are or how well or badly your life is going.

Your feelings only ever do that one thing: reflect thought in the moment. Feel the feeling, of stress or whatever it is, and wait it out. Don't be afraid of it. It can't hurt you. A new feeling will come along in a moment, and it will most likely bring you the "a-ha!" you need to move forward.

Q. I want to learn more about the principles behind the "A-ha!" Method. How do I do that?

A. I'm always available to answer questions, and I offer coaching and workshops to help you or your team solve problems with greater ease. Find me online at www.maryschiller.com or www.ahabook.biz. Feel free to get in touch with me: mary@maryschiller.com.

What's next? Well, I'd sure love for you to ...

CHAPTER 7:
SHARE YOUR "A-HA!"

You have unique insights and "a-ha!" discoveries every day, and I'd love to hear about them.

1) Your review of this short book on Amazon or wherever you purchased it (thank you!) would be so appreciated. Many, many thanks.

2) If this book has been valuable to you, please share it on social media, or give a copy to a friend or loved one. You might find people in your workplace, your neighborhood, your place of worship or your child's school who could benefit, too.

3) Tweet @MaryJSchiller and share your personal "a-ha!"; I would love to hear about it!

4) Subscribe online at www.ahabook.biz to learn more about upcoming A-ha! Method classes, workshops for businesses and personalized coaching. You can also find me at www.maryschiller.com.

Thank you for reading and sharing *A-ha! How to solve any problem in record time.*

Much love to you,
Mary

THE END … OF ENDLESS PROBLEMS

ABOUT THE AUTHOR

Mary Schiller is an author and coach who helps people experience more joy, relaxation and clarity in their lives.

She is also the author of *The Joy Formula: The simple equation that will change your life*; and *Mind Yoga: The simple solution to stress that you've never heard before*.

Before she began coaching people and writing books, Mary taught university students how to write the perfect essay. Later, she became a communications officer at Columbia University, crafting messages for the business and medical schools. She holds advanced degrees in English and in education.

A native Californian, Mary loves the sun and the surf but also enjoys traveling, particularly to Europe, the UK and Costa Rica. She's passionate about classical music (Beethoven is unmatched), art, photography and knitting, particularly sweaters. She's married and has a grown daughter plus two adorable cats. While Mary and her husband currently live in New York City, they may be making a move across the Atlantic very soon. Wherever she may be, you can find and connect with Mary online at www.maryschiller.com.

Printed in Great Britain
by Amazon